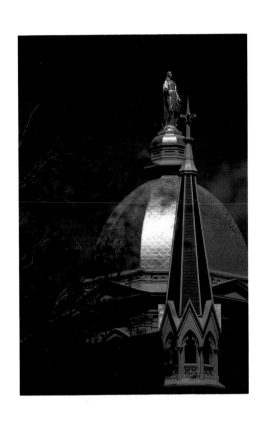

THE UNIVERSITY OF

NOTRE DAME du LAC

Notre Dame

A SENSE OF PLACE

Photographed by William Strode

HARMONY HOUSE PUBLISHERS - LOUISVILLE
In cooperation with the
UNIVERSITY OF NOTRE DAME PRESS

Our thanks to the University of Notre Dame for all its help in the production of this book.
In particular we wish to thank Richard Conklin, Bruce Harlan, Jaime Cripe, Vince Wehby Jr., John Heisler,
Jethrow Kyles, Charles Lennon, James Langford, Charles Lamb, Thomas Schlereth and James Murphy.

Executive Editors: William Butler and William Strode
Library of Congress Catalog Number 87-083173
Hardcover International Standard Book Number 0-916509-35
Printed in U.S.A. by Pinaire Lithographing Corp., Louisville, Kentucky
First Edition November 1988
Published by Harmony House Publishers, P.O. Box 90, Prospect, Kentucky 40059
(502)228-2010 / 228-4446
Distributed by the University of Notre Dame Press
for the Notre Dame Alumni Association.

Introduction by Michael Garvey
Additional photography by Bruce Harlan, pages 22-23; Vince Wehby Jr., pages 72, 83 and 97.

Rev. Edward Sorin, C.S.C.

11

Preceeding Page: Sacred Heart Church

14

PREFACE

For those nurtured on its campus and proud of its traditions and spirit, Notre Dame evokes a sense of family. Whatever one's origins or time of matriculation or employment, there is a bond that links the generations and makes them comfortable with the symbols, sites and songs of the place.

The central mission, of course, is educational. Notre Dame is a center of teaching and research where the privileged interaction between professor and student, researcher and colleague, is supported and sustained. Its administration and faculty alike are challenged to combine technical competence with moral vision; to appreciate the intellectual and international context of modern political, economic and social relations; to open up the world of the future without forgetting the cultural roots upon which real progress is built.

Indeed, Notre Dame is a university in the full American sense, with its traditions of academic freedom, scholarly inquiry and peer review. Yet it aspires to be something more, for it is a Catholic university. This entails broader and deeper vision than the secular academy sometimes allows. Here the pursuit of truth is seen as a genuine route to God. While there are no questions that cannot be asked, there are certain values and perspectives that have pride of place. The richness of the Catholic tradition with its stress on a sacramental sense of God's presence and the inseparable connection between faith and reason, spirit and flesh, grace and nature, includes all realms of human endeavor.

The Catholicity of Notre Dame is captured by no one dimension of its common life. It includes the academic curriculum with required undergraduate courses in theology and philosophy, the value-oriented research that takes place, the opportunities for social service participation, the outreach programs serving the Church at large, and, of course, the worship life of the campus.

Much of the loyalty of its graduates is forged in their experience of the residential life of the campus. Each residence hall has a specific mystique and set of traditions. Through the staff's attentive and concerned leadership in the hall and the whole range of services available under the Office of Student Affairs, Notre Dame attempts to promote the growth of the whole person – in worship and in relationship, in career choices and in responses to the normal crises of life. The fun of dances, the thrill of intercollegiate and intramural athletic competition, and the increasing cultural opportunities all make for a rich and fulfilling life.

There is much to cherish in Notre Dame's history – the dedicated and continued presence of its Holy Cross community of priests and brothers; the smooth transition to a primarily lay Board of Trustees, and its national and international visibility as America's best-known Catholic university.

Even reflection on the challenges that lie ahead give one reason for hope. Notre Dame will become even more diverse in the backgrounds and identities of those who study and work here without sacrificing the loyalty and support of those who have enjoyed its benefits in the past. Its clearly articulated institutional mission inspires the financial support necessary for it to flourish. Finally, it can focus its resources so that students and faculty are properly prepared for wise and thoughtful participation in matters of civil and ecclesial policy. It is uniquely situated, in continuity with the vision of its founder, to serve both society and the Church.

Edward A. Malloy, CSC

INTRODUCTION

By Michael Garvey

There was some attractive lake land in the Potawatomi, Miami and Chippewa mission fields of New France. Pere Marquette had probably passed through the area in 1675 on his way home from Illinois to the Jesuit mission at St. Ignace, and La Salle's access to the Mississippi had surely obliged him to follow the natives' customary portage between the St. Joseph River and the headwaters of the Kankakee. The portage trail ran through a thin forest from which, two centuries later, a golden dome would be visible. In 1686, a French Jesuit named Claude Allouez established a mission to the Potawatomi people here and named it Sainte Marie des Lacs. After Allouez came other missionaries; Stephen Badin, who was the first priest ordained in the new nation, and Louis De Seille, his Belgian successor, whose health broke in his thirty-seventh year, and Benjamin Petit, who accompanied and thus earned the affection of the few Potawatomi survivors of that people's forcible and nearly genocidal exile to the west in 1839.

And then came Edward Sorin, a boundlessly energetic 28-year-old Breton priest of a newly formed order, the Congregation of Holy Cross. In 1836, at the seminary in Le Mans, he had met Simon Brute, the Bishop of Vincennes, and heard the stories of Allouez, Badin, De Seille and Petit. Six years later, on November 26, Sorin and a band of seven Holy Cross brothers arrived at the shore of St. Mary's lake to take possession of 524 acres so blanketed by snow that the nearby St. Joseph lake was invisible. It was for Sorin, as it would be for thousands and thousands of his followers, a case of love at first sight. "Everything was frozen," he wrote back to the Holy Cross community in France, "and yet the landscape appeared so beautiful. The lake, with its mantle of resplendent white snow, was to us a symbol of the purity of Our Lady, whose name it bears and also of the purity of soul which should characterize the new inhabitants of these lovely shores."

Whether or not those new inhabitants of the area he named *Notre Dame du Lac* lived up to Sorin's exuberant vision, they quickly got down to his business. They had $300 cash, a short credit line, and an indefatigable chief executive with a profoundly unrealistic ambition for which he was nevertheless able to enlist enthusiastic support. Instead of a winter campground beside a pretty lake on the Indiana frontier, Sorin saw a community of scholars at work on a shrine to the Mother of God. An arguably romantic vision, it was borne along for years solely by Sorin's shrewd sense and iron will. Whatever reservations fellow pioneers may have had about this enigmatic French newcomer and his plans, within two years the Indiana legislature had been persuaded to charter the University of Notre Dame du Lac.

Advertisements began to appear in America's nineteenth century media for an institution boasting "all of the advantages of convenience, attractive scenery, pure and invigorating air, and excellent springs" which formed "not only a beautiful abode, but also an agreeable solitude, which facilitates so effectually the intellectual improvement of youth." The advertisements informed those interested that the new institution's faculty was comprised entirely of Holy Cross priests, but assured families of potential students of other faiths that "there will be no interference with their religious tenets; they will be required only to attend the religious excercises with decorum, this being in conformity with the

Rev. William Corby, C.S.C.

rules of all Catholic colleges in the United States."

What Sorin insisted upon calling a "University" from the moment he arrived here existed largely in his fertile imagination. A more objective observer might have called it a pioneer boarding school. In subsequent years it grew into an internationally prestigious and materially prosperous institution of higher learning. A person of Sorin's daunting self-confidence and creative impatience would simply expect such growth as the natural fruit of a good idea. Those hampered by more sluggish ambitions might find it remarkable that in 1844 Notre Dame's yearly tuition was $100. Room and board was $65 extra. There were eight faculty members, twenty-five students, five buildings, a few chickens and a corn crop. And, of course, two mesmerizing lakes.

The two lakes are physical and imaginative fixtures in Notre Dame landscape. The yellow brick with which Sorin and his company built so much of the old campus is kilned clay from the lake floors, although one fondly remembered faculty member, Frank O'Malley, later said that there was blood in those bricks, too. There was during Sorin's time a University rule requiring all summer students to bathe in common, twice a week, in St. Joseph's lake—a regulation obviating the rule which required them, during the winter months, to wash their feet once a week. For countless members of what is still unabashedly called the Notre Dame family, a primitive childhood memory of the place involves a stroll with parents, a bagful of breadcrumbs and a lakeside encounter with ducks. The foundational love for thousands of families, religious vows, and forms of selfgiving more difficult to categorize has been received or discovered during strolls around the lakes. And, like the University's students, faculty, administration and staff, visitors and returning alumni find it impossible to stay away from the lakes very long.

Since the day an exultant Sorin and his friends placed their vision and their swath of frozen Indiana wilderness under the protection of Our Lady, Notre Dame, whether thought of as a university, a place, a gathering of generations or all three of these things, has been the beneficiary of what Professor Edward Fischer called "a long-descending blessing." Beginning that day, Notre Dame has played an irreplaceable role in the affairs of the Church, nation and world. It has often been a glorious role, ample with heroism. One thinks of the courage and compassion of Father William Corby's ministry amid the carnage of Gettysburg; the unyielding intellectual integrity of Fathers John Zahm and Julius Nieuwland; Knute Rockne's inspirational exuberance; Dr. Tom Dooley's singlehearted devotion to the poor of Southeast Asia and his cheerfully accepted death.

To all these heroes, the words spoken by University president Father Charles O'Donnell during Knute Rockne's funeral could equally apply. "He made use of all the proper machinery and legitimate methods of modern activity to be essentially not modern at all," Father O'Donnell said. "To be quite elementarily human and Christian, giving himself, spending himself, like water, not for himself, but for others. And once again, in his case, most illustriously is verified the Christian paradox—he has cast away to keep, he has lost his life to find it. This is not death, but immortality."

The paradox at the center of its community has made Notre Dame, during its finest moments, a place of peculiarly Catholic hospitality to which any soul open and honest enough could fairly lay claim. G.K. Chesterton noticed and spoke about this years ago. On his first visit to America, Chesterton said, he had been struck by the country's enormity and distance from what was familar and dear to him. "I did not feel like that at all when I came to America the second time," he told the Notre Dame students he had come to teach. "If you want to know why I felt different, the reason is in the name of your University. That name was quite sufficient as far as I was concerned. It would not have mattered if it had been in the mountains of the moon. Where she has erected her pillars, all men are at home, and I knew that I should not find strangers."

During the first quarter of this century, that name would be suffice as well for generations of Irish, Italian, Polish and Hispanic Catholic immigrants who loudly cheered and bitterly mourned the victories and defeats of a football team on whose campus many of them had never set foot.

It was also during the first quarter of the century that Father James A. Burns, the University's tenth president, made a visionary and controversial decision to close Notre Dame's "preparatory" department. Burns' decision to reorganize Notre Dame academically left in its wake many of the present administrative contours of the University and made possible the distinction it enjoys today.

Colleagues said Father Burns gave small thought to the present, so great was his preoccupation with the future. It fell to this successor, Father Matthew Walsh, to harmonize the University's physical plant with its new academic shape. Walsh oversaw the construction of the South Dining Hall and the great dormitories like Howard, Morrissey, and Lyons Halls.

While enabling widespread access to the vision of which Sorin had spoken and which men like Burns and Walsh had begun to realize, Notre Dame's particularly colorful football tradition, by the middle of the century, had threatened to eclipse Sorin's shared dream of a great Catholic university. Father John Cavanaugh and his successor, Father Theodore Hesburgh, prodded what might have become a parochial complacence toward the restless spirit of the University's origins. During his 35-year tenure and with a tenacity equal to that of Fathers Burns, Walsh and Cavanaugh, Hesburgh dramatically increased Notre Dame's endowment, expanded its physical plant, enriched its faculty and student body (the University became coeducational in 1972) and greatly improved the quality of graduate education and research. But Notre Dame remained a community of inquiry where scholars and believers revered

spiritual values as well as facts.

The Hesburgh era, for all its explosive growth, change and even occasional controversy, was more rediscovery than rejection of the tradition of a community which an independent and determined French priest established on an Indiana lakeshore. Father Hesburgh's valedictory resonates with an older vision. "If we are faithful to our Catholic heritage and our dedication to Our Lady in this place," he said in May 1987, "the future may well make the past look dull and uneventful. All great universities are by their very natures splendid places where truth reigns supreme, truth which is another name for God, the Transcendent, the Immense, the Holy. Add to that natural truth, common to all universities, the basic truth of faith, truth beyond knowing spoken to us by the Holy Spirit through the prophets and evangelists, truth treasured above all else by the Church, truth incarnate in Jesus Christ, Our Lord, then one truly adds to the splendor of the place. Now we speak of eternal meanings and divine realities added to the natural treasure of the university. Now we envision grace elevating nature to the divine, eternity transcending time, substance substituted for shadow."

The splendor of which both presidents Sorin and Hesburgh often spoke has nothing to do with institutional wealth, international reputation and powerful influence. The long-descending blessing which ignited Sorin's enthusiasm was as accessible to the Notre Dame family in the hardscrabble early days as it is in the far more comfortable present. It was there from the first night Sorin made camp: "Yes, we are happy," he wrote back to his brothers in France. "We have the Lord with us. Only tonight, we hung our sanctuary lamp where none had hung before...They tell us we won't be able to afford to keep it burning. But we have a little olive oil and will burn it while it lasts...We can see it as we come through the woods, and it lights the humble home where our Master dwells. We tell each other that we are not alone, that Jesus Christ lives among us. It gives us courage."

Medieval Institute

UNIVERSITY OF NOTRE DAME

1679 Robert Sieur de La Salle establishes Fort Miami one half mile west of the present Notre Dame Campus.

1680-86 Father Claude Allouez and Father Claude D'Ablon establish St. Joseph Mission on the banks of the St. Joseph River above the portage at South Bend.

1830 Chief Leopold Pokagon of the Potawatomi Indians asks the Bishop of Detroit to send a missionary to northern Indiana. Father Stephen Badin is sent and opens a mission near South Bend.

1840 Rev. Basil A. Moreau founds the Congregation of Holy Cross in France.

1842 Rev. Edward F. Sorin, a member of the new religious community, arrives at Badin's mission with the intention of opening a school.

1843 First building (now known as Old College) is constructed on the University campus.

1844 Notre Dame is granted a charter by the State of Indiana.

1849 Neal Gillespie and Richard Shortis become Notre Dame's first graduates and go on to become Holy Cross priests.

1855 Rev. Philip Foley of Toledo gives the University $4,000 to establish its first scholarship fund.

1863 Rev. William Corby, C.S.C., grants general absolution to Union troops at the Battle of Gettysburg.

1867 *The Scholastic Years* (later *The Notre Dame Scholastic*) begins publication.

1868 The Alumni Association is founded.

1869 Notre Dame Law School opens as first Catholic law school in the country.

1871 Cornerstone of Sacred Heart Church is laid.

1873 Notre Dame becomes first Catholic school in America to offer a course in engineering.

1879 Fire destroys the University's Main Building, which is rebuilt the same year.

1883 John Gilmary Shea is awarded the first Laetare Medal.

1887 Notre Dame plays its first intercollegiate football game and loses 8-0 to the University of Michigan.

1888 Sorin Hall is built as the first Catholic college residence hall with private rooms.

1893 Father Sorin, founder, first president, and first chairman of the Board of Trustees, dies at age 79.

1895 Prof. Jerome Green becomes the first American to send a wireless message.

1896 Rev. John Zahm, C.S.C., publishes *Evolution and Dogma*, in which he

A SELECTED CHRONOLOGY

makes the controversial assertion that there is no contradiction between the theory of evolution and Catholicism.

1897 The University divides its administration into four colleges: Arts and Letters, Science, Engineering, and Law. (The College of Business Administration was established in 1921.)

1906 Replica of Father Stephen Badin's original log chapel is constructed.

1917 Lemonnier Library (now the Architecture Building) is constructed.

1918 Summer school is instituted.

1919 Rev. James A. Burns, C.S.C., is elected president and brings major changes in the school's academics and administration.

1920 Father Burns appoints a twelve-man Board of Associate Lay Trustees, which is advisory.

1921 The Rockefeller and Carnegie Foundations provide matching funds for the first major endowment drive.

1923 A Ku Klux Klan march through South Bend meets opposition from students.

1924 The Four Horsemen lead Notre Dame to its first official national football championship.

1929 Notre Dame closes its grade school.

1931 Father Julius A. Nieuwland's chemical research discoveries leading to

synthetic rubber are announced.

1931 Football coach Knute Rockne dies in a plane crash.

1934 Father (later Cardinal) John O'Hara becomes Notre Dame's president.

1939 Notre Dame physicists, using homemade "atom smasher," are first to disintegrate the nucleus by electron bombardment.

1941 A unit of the Naval Reserve Officers Training Corps, the first of what will be ROTC training by all three armed services, is established. Between 1942-46, almost 12,000 naval officers will be trained at Notre Dame.

1946 "Vetville" is built to house married World War II veterans returning to school.

1952 Rev. Theodore M. Hesburgh, C.S.C., is named president.

1960 Ford Foundation picks Notre Dame as one of five American universities described as "regional centers of academic excellence," first of successive multimillion dollar fund-raising campaigns is launched.

1963 Memorial Library (now Hesburgh Library) is built.

1967 Changeover to lay governance is effected with creation of Fellows of the University and predominantly lay Board of Trustees.

1972 Notre Dame goes coeducational on the undergraduate level.

1987 Rev. Edward A. Malloy, C.S.C., is chosen sixteenth president.

I walked that early September, among the old brick buildings tinged with yellow and partly hidden by ivy, and marveled at leaded windows and slate roofs with their blue-grey cast. I failed to notice, though, how the old French section and the collegiate Gothic blend because of massed greenery of oak, maple, birch, sycamore and pine.

Edward Fischer, *Notre Dame Remembered*, 1987

Rockne Memorial

Overleaf : Hurley College of Business Administration

Law School

Shaheen-Mestrovic Memorial

His snug little chamber is crammed in all nooks
With worthless old knicknacks and silly old books,
And foolish old odds and foolish old ends,
Cracked bargains from brokers, cheap keepsakes from friends.
Old armor, prints, pictures, pipes, china (all cracked),
Old rickety tables and chairs broken-backed,
A two-penny treasury, wondrous to see;
What matter? 'Tis pleasant to you, friend, and me.

Paul Fenlon's description of a bachelor don's room
in the 1907 *Dome*

Overleaf: Grace and Flanner Towers

Sorin Hall

There's blood in the bricks.

Francis J. O'Malley

Lyons Arch

Sorin Hall

Overleaf: Hayes-Healy Courtyard

43

Moses Statue

An enormous, complex thing, that Christian tradition. It is the cultural aspect of faith.
At its simplest it seems to consist of a double awareness: a realization of God, humanly
incarnate; and a realization of man, unspeakably dignified at this divine sharing of his nature.
Peculiar, unique, it draws heavily upon Judiac and Greek – indeed upon all human –
preparations. It is supernatural: which does not mean that it ignores the natural,
but that it goes beyond it, above it. It contains immense moral and spiritual implications;
it has a power of penetrating, impregnating, energizing. It is intellectual, cultural, and religious.
It furnishes at Notre Dame an atmosphere, a very air, in which work is done. Not that out
of a germ-free cage at Lobund there will ever emerge a Christian guinea pig; or that in the
Mathematical Department here there is any theological talk about points, lines, or polygons.
But insofar as work is affected by the surrounding climate in which it is done, no work here
carried on lies outside the intense influence of the surrounding tradition.

Richard Sullivan, in *Notre Dame: Reminiscences of an Era*, 1951

Parents send us their young because they still believe that this is a special place, a place with an intimate chemistry between student and teacher, and between those two and God Almighty. While concerned that their offspring acquire employable skills, these parents trust that their children will also be marked by encounters with passionate souls who love learning and beauty for themselves, and who love the faith of their fathers.

Robert Leader, in *Reflections in the Dome*, 1985

Sacred Heart Church

Overleaf: Law School Diploma Ceremony   57

The Grotto

AT NOTRE DAME

So well I love these woods I half believe
There is an intimate fellowship we share;
So many years we breathed the same air,
Kept spring in common, and were one to grieve
Summer's undoing, saw the fall bereave
Us both of beauty, together learned to bear
The weight of winter – when I would go otherwhere –
An unreturning journey – I would leave
Some whisper of a song in these old oaks;
A football lingering 'till some distant Summer
Another singer down these paths may stray –
The destined one a gold future cloaks –
And he may love them, too, this graced newcomer
And may remember that I passed this way.

Rev. Charles O'Donnell, C.S.C., *Collected Poems*, 1942

An Tostal

Bookstore Basketball

Overleaf: Women's Field Hockey

Bengal Bouts

Washington Hall

As regards this 'seeing things whole," anything at all will do as a starting point, although admittedly some things do better than other things. A human person does better than anything. I myself like to start with: a pebble, or a ripple in a stream, or a blade of grass, or a rose, or a sapling, or a robin redbreast, or a star, or a starlet, or telestar, or a whisp of hair, or a smile, or a jet (an "ordinary" jet), or a Concorde supersonic jet, or a "Jet-Pak," or a "whirling dervish," or a "surrey with the fringe on top," or a family, or a village, or a body politic, or a "flash in the pan," or a "Jack of all trades," or "someone crazy enough to give me a daisy."

Joseph Evans in "A Search for Wholeness," *Scholastic*, 1975

I was present when Father Sorin, after looking over the destruction of his life's work, stood at the altar steps and spoke to the community what I have always felt to be the most sublime words I have ever listened to. There was absolute faith, confidence, resolution in his very look and pose. "If it were all gone, I should not give up," were his words in closing. The effect was electric. It was the crowning moment of his life. A sad company had gone into the church that day. They were all simple Christian heroes when they came out. There was never more a shadow of a doubt as to the future of Notre Dame.

Professor Timothy Howard describing the aftermath of the 1879 Main Building fire

Notre Dame Marching Band

Outlined against a blue-gray October sky, the Four Horsemen rode again. In dramatic lore, they are known as Famine, Pestilence, Destruction and Death. These are only aliases. Their real names are Stuhldreher, Miller, Crowley and Layden. They formed the crest of the South Bend Cyclone before another fighting Army football team was swept over the precipice at the Polo Grounds yesterday afternoon as 55,000 spectators peered down on the bewildering panorama spread on the green plain below.

Grantland Rice describing Notre Dame versus Army in 1924

I'VE GOT TO GO, ROCK. IT'S ALL RIGHT.
I'M NOT AFRAID SOMETIME ROCK,
WHEN THE TEAM'S UP AGAINST IT.
WHEN THINGS ARE WRONG AND THE
BREAKS ARE BEATING THE BOYS.
TELL THEM TO GO IN THERE WITH ALL
THEY'VE GOT AND WIN JUST ONE FOR
THE GIPPER. I DON'T KNOW WHERE I'LL
BE THEN ROCK. BUT I'LL KNOW ABOUT
IT, AND I'LL BE HAPPY.

Words from George Gipp

Cheer, cheer for old Notre Dame
Wake up the echoes cheering her name,
Send a volley cheer on high
Shake down the thunder from the sky...

From the *Notre Dame Victory March*

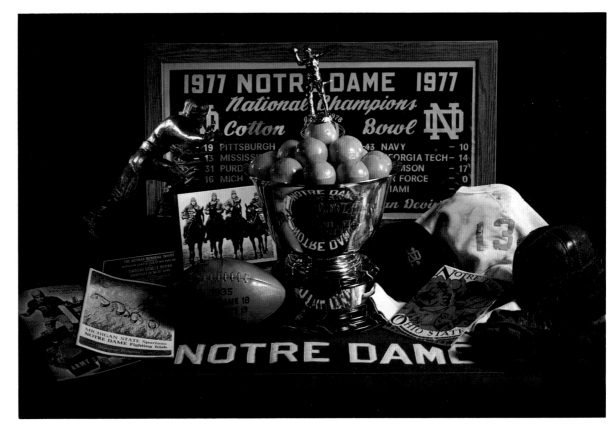

Overleaf: The Hesburgh Library

Ship atop Hurley College of Business Administration

Mestrovic Gallery 101

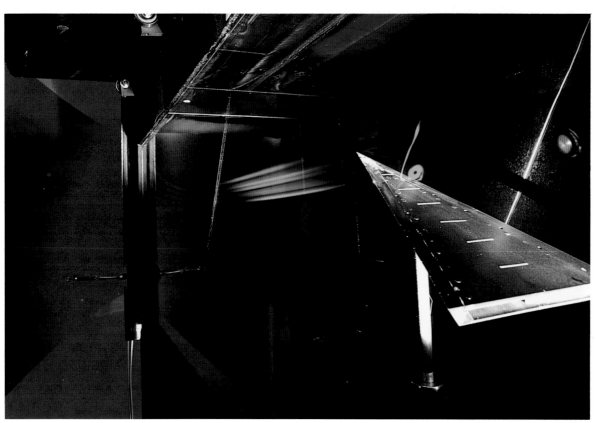

Wind Tunnel

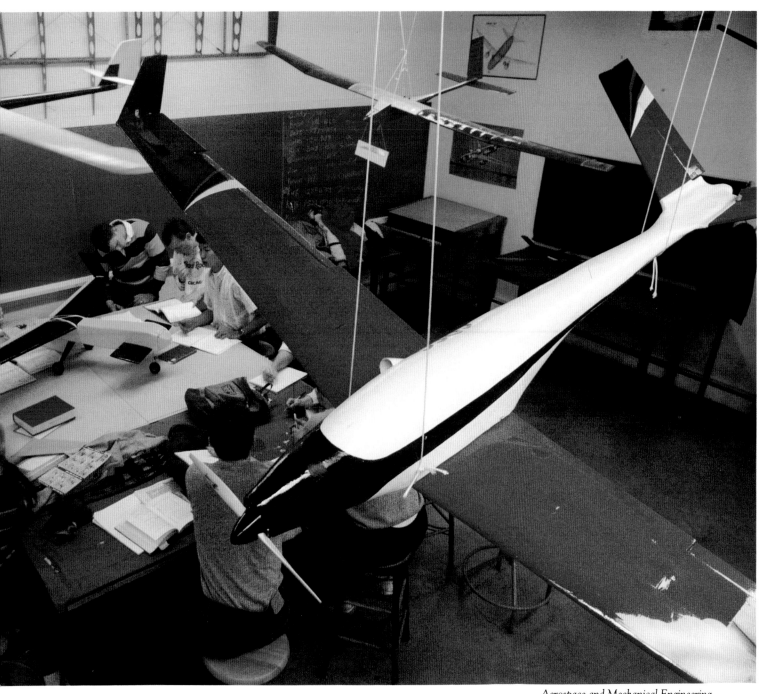

Aerospace and Mechanical Engineering

Clarke Memorial Fountain

Baccalaureate Mass

Overleaf: Commencement

107

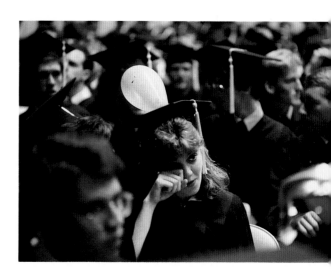

University Mace

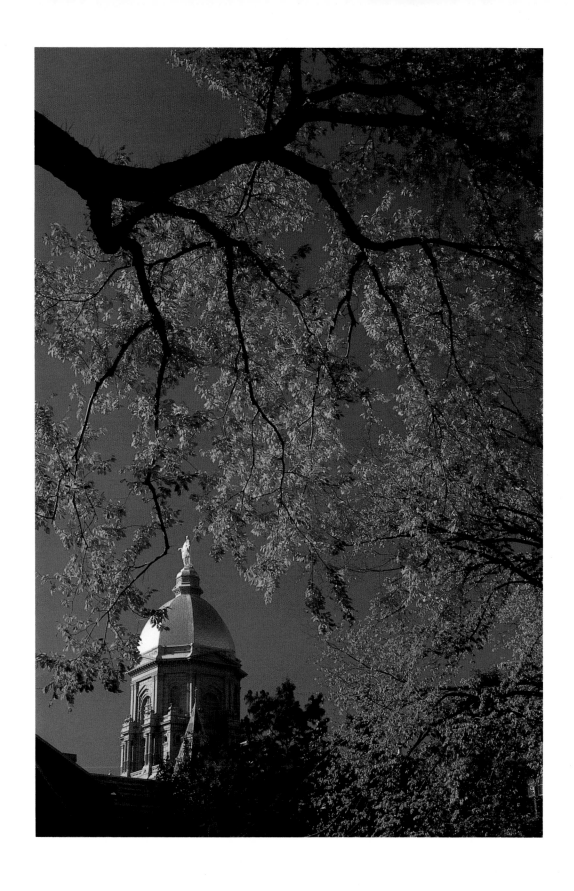

Alma Mater

Notre Dame, Our Mother, tender, strong and true
Proudly in the heavens gleams thy gold and blue.
Glory's mantle cloaks thee, golden is thy fame
And our hearts forever praise thee, Notre Dame:
And our hearts forever love thee, Notre Dame.